GROUNDHOG HIBERNATION

by Martha London

Consultant: Beth Gambro
Reading Specialist, Yorkville, Illinois

Minneapolis, Minnesota

Teaching Tips

Before Reading

- Look at the cover of the book. Discuss the picture and the title.
- Ask readers to brainstorm a list of what they already know about groundhogs. What can they expect to see in this book?
- Go on a picture walk, looking through the pictures to discuss vocabulary and make predictions about the text.

During Reading

- Read for purpose. Encourage readers to think about groundhog hibernation as they are reading.
- Ask readers to look for the details of the book. What do groundhogs do to get ready to hibernate?
- If readers encounter an unknown word, ask them to look at the sounds in the word. Then, ask them to look at the rest of the page. Are there any clues to help them understand?

After Reading

- Encourage readers to pick a buddy and reread the book together.
- Ask readers to name one reason groundhogs sleep. Find the page that tells about this thing.
- Ask readers to write or draw something they learned about groundhog hibernation.

Credits:
Cover and title page, © arlutz73/iStock; 3, © vagabond54/Shutterstock; 5, © Brian E Kushner/Shutterstock; 7TL, © romrodinka/iStock; 7TR, © Drake Fleege/iStock; 7BL, © Wildnerdpix/iStock; 7BR, © Kyle Selcer/Adobe Stock; 8-9, © shaunl/iStock; 11, © JamesBrey/iStock; 12-13, © Karel Bock/iStock; 15, © coyotepics/iStock; 16-17, © Dominique Braud/Dembinsky Photo Associates/Alamy / Alamy Stock Photo/Alamy; 19, © David P. Lewis/Shutterstock; 20-21, © Jeramey Lende/Adobe Stock; 22T, © Mircea Costina/Shutterstock; 22ML, © Jeramey Lende/Shutterstock; 22MR, © Paul Reeves Photography/Shutterstock; 22B, © Dominique Braud/Dembinsky Photo Associates/Alamy / Alamy Stock Photo/Alamy; 23TL, © kotopalych/Adobe Stock; 23TM, © New Africa/Adobe Stock; 23TR, © Camille Lamoureux/Adobe Stock; 23BL, © Ysbrand Cosijn/Shutterstock; 23BR, © OlegDoroshin/Shutterstock and © leolintang/Shutterstock.

STATEMENT ON USAGE OF GENERATIVE ARTIFICIAL INTELLIGENCE
Bearport Publishing remains committed to publishing high-quality nonfiction books. Therefore, we restrict the use of generative AI to ensure accuracy of all text and visual components pertaining to a book's subject. See BearportPublishing.com for details.

Library of Congress Cataloging-in-Publication Data

Names: London, Martha, author. | Gambro, Beth, consultant.
Title: Groundhog hibernation / by Martha London ; consultant Beth Gambro, Reading Specialist.
Description: Minneapolis, Minnesota : Bearport Publishing Company, [2024] | Series: Weather makes them sleep | Includes bibliographical references and index.
Identifiers: LCCN 2023028921 (print) | LCCN 2023028922 (ebook) | ISBN 9798889162247 (hardcover) | ISBN 9798889162292 (paperback) | ISBN 9798889162339 (ebook)
Subjects: LCSH: Woodchuck--Juvenile literature. | Woodchuck--Hibernation--Juvenile literature.
Classification: LCC QL737.R68 L6238 2024 (print) | LCC QL737.R68 (ebook) | DDC 599.36/61565--dc23/eng/20230713
LC record available at https://lccn.loc.gov/2023028921
LC ebook record available at https://lccn.loc.gov/2023028922

For more information, write to Bearport Publishing, 5357 Penn Avenue South, Minneapolis, MN 55419.

Contents

Time to Sleep 4

Eat, Dig, Rest 22

Glossary 23

Index 24

Read More 24

Learn More Online 24

About the Author 24

Time to Sleep

Brr!

Winter is on the way.

A groundhog is busy in its **burrow**.

What is the groundhog getting ready for?

Groundhogs live in places that have four **seasons**.

Each season has different weather.

Some are warmer.

Others are colder.

The weather is hot during the summer.

Groundhogs spend this time digging their winter homes.

They need a very deep burrow for the cold.

Groundhogs also eat a lot of food in the summer.

They munch on tall grass.

They eat fruit and tree bark, too.

The weather gets colder in the fall.

Plants stop growing.

It is hard for groundhogs to find food.

Groundhogs head to their deep burrows for winter.

Here, they stay warm while they snooze.

They sleep through the cold weather on beds of dry grass.

As groundhogs sleep, their body **temperatures** go down.

Their heartbeats slow, too.

This helps them save **energy**.

Groundhogs sleep for up to six months.

They do not eat at all during this time.

Then, the weather gets warmer.

Soon, there are plenty of new spring plants to eat.

It is time for the groundhogs to get up!

Eat, Dig, Rest

Summer

Groundhogs dig their winter burrows. They eat plants.

Fall

Groundhogs move into their winter burrows.

Winter

Groundhogs sleep. Their heartbeats slow. Their body temperatures drop.

Spring

Weather gets warmer. Groundhogs wake up.

Glossary

burrow a hole or tunnel dug by an animal to live in

energy the power needed by all living things to be active and stay alive

seasons the parts of the year with different weather

temperatures how hot or cold things are

Index

burrow 4, 9, 14, 22
dig 9, 22
food 10, 12
grass 10, 16
seasons 6
sleep 4, 14, 16, 18, 22
weather 6, 9, 12, 14, 18, 22

Read More

Banks, Rosie. *Why Do Animals Hibernate? (Why Do Animals Do That?).* New York: Gareth Stevens Publishing, 2024.

London, Martha. *Groundhogs (Underground Animals).* Minneapolis: Pop!, 2021.

Learn More Online

1. Go to **www.factsurfer.com** or scan the QR code below.
2. Enter **"Groundhog Hibernation"** into the search box.
3. Click on the cover of this book to see a list of websites.

About the Author

Martha London loves writing about animals! She has two cats. They love to sleep in the sun.